W9-APR-718

ISIS

HOSTAGES

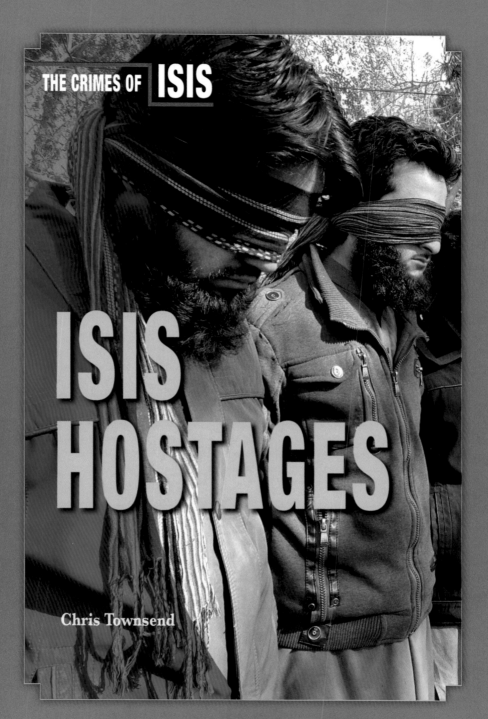

THE CRIMES OF **ISIS**

ISIS HOSTAGES

Chris Townsend

Enslow Publishing
101 W. 23rd Street
Suite 240
New York, NY 10011
USA

enslow.com

Published in 2018 by Enslow Publishing, LLC.
101 W. 23rd Street, Suite 240, New York, NY 10011

Copyright © 2018 by Enslow Publishing, LLC.

All rights reserved.

No part of this book may be reproduced by any means
without the written permission of the publisher.

Library of Congress Cataloging-in-Publication Data

Names: Townsend, Chris (Writer on the Middle East), author.
Title: ISIS hostages / by Chris Townsend.
Description: New York : Enslow Publishing, 2018. | Series: The crimes of ISIS |
  Includes bibliographical references and index. | Audience: Grades 7–12.
Identifiers: LCCN 2017020072 | ISBN 9780766092174 (library bound) | ISBN
  9780766095854 (paperback)
Subjects: LCSH: IS (Organization)—Juvenile literature. | Terrorism—Juvenile
  literature. | Hostages—Juvenile literature.
Classification: LCC HV6433.I722 T693 2018 | DDC 363.325—dc23
LC record available at https://lccn.loc.gov/2017020072

Printed in the United States of America

To Our Readers: We have done our best to make sure all website addresses in
this book were active and appropriate when we went to press. However, the author
and the publisher have no control over and assume no liability for the material
available on those websites or on any websites they may link to. Any comments or
suggestions can be sent by email to customerservice@enslow.com.

Photo Credits: Cover, pp. 3, 28, 81, 88–89 Anadolu Agency/Getty Images;
pp. 6, 66 Safin Hamed/AFP/Getty Images; pp. 8–9 Salah Malkawi/Getty
Images; p. 13 Interim Archives/Archive Photos/Getty Images; p. 16 Express/
Archive Photos/Getty Images; p. 19 ZUMA Press, Inc./Alamy Stock Photo;
pp. 20–21 Rex Features/AP Images; p. 23 Daily Courier/AP Images; pp. 26,
40 © AP Images; pp. 32–33 Kevin Frayer/Getty Images; p. 35 Valerie Macon/
AFP/Getty Images; pp. 38–39 STR/AFP/Getty Images; pp. 42–43 Joel Saget/
AFP/Getty Images; pp. 46–47 Charly Triballeau/AFP/Getty Images; pp. 50–51
Alexander Koerner/Getty Images; p. 54 Reuters/Newscom; p. 57 Alamy Stock
Photo; pp. 60–61 Ilyas Dean/Hulton Archive/Getty Images; pp. 62–63 Carl
Court/Getty Images; p. 69 Yoshikazu Tsuno/AFP/Getty Images; pp. 72–73
NurPhoto/Getty Images; pp. 76–77 © Spc. Tristan Bolden/Planet Pix/ZUMA
Wire; pp. 84–85 Karim Sahib/AFP/Getty Images.

CONTENTS

Introduction 7

A Storied Tradition 10

Stranger in a Strange Land 18

Taking All Comers 27

On Foreign Soil 36

Cities Under Siege 49

Interpreting God's Will 58

Free at Last 68

Strategy of Fear 80

Chapter Notes 91

Glossary 97

Further Reading 101

Index 102

INTRODUCTION

The Islamic State of Iraq and Syria (ISIS), also known as the Islamic State of Iraq and the Levant (ISIL), or simply the Islamic State (IS), rose from the ashes of al-Qaeda in Iraq (AQI) around 2014. The brutality of the group and its attacks against other Muslims have led parent organization al-Qaeda, the perpetrator of the September 11, 2001, attacks on the United States, to disown the group as too violent. One of the hallmarks of the group is its gruesome videos, wherein it beheads hostages in front of a camera, usually with a message of warning for Western countries.

The group has taken hostages from all walks of life. Journalists who are trying to tell the story of the wars in Syria and Iraq have been frequent targets of ISIS, as have aid workers from foreign countries just trying to help those caught in the conflict. Beyond foreigners, ISIS has taken hostages from among the populace it controls, whether they be Muslims from a different sect, Christians, or other religions deemed pagan. The group has reached beyond its borders and taken hostages throughout the world in so-called lone-wolf attacks executed on ISIS's behalf.

The costs of this campaign of terror have been steep, damaging tourism revenues in many countries from France to Egypt. People are afraid that they might end up a captive of the group and star in its latest video. The group uses its hostages for a variety of reasons. Some of the hostages are used as propaganda, the gruesome killings a warning to others and a symbol of the group's strength. These hostage videos have proven to be powerful recruitment tools, drawing thousands from other countries to fight for ISIS.

A common feature in hostage situations throughout history is demands made against local political systems, but ISIS seems to revel in the killing of hostages for killing's sake. The quality of their videography and special effects show a level of sophistication never seen from a terrorist group before. Combined with videos of battles and daily life in the caliphate, the hostage videos are a powerful tool that ISIS uses to shape its narrative of a war with the West—one that it claims to be winning.

Reality could not be further from the truth. ISIS is losing ground on every front. Iraqi soldiers are driving ISIS from the city of Mosul in Iraq, while Syrian and Kurdish forces are moving closer to the ISIS capital in Raqqa, Syria.

In addition to the war against ISIS, Syrians are currently embroiled in a civil war that has been raging for years. Here, Syrians in Jordan protest against Syrian president Bashar al-Assad in 2011.

The danger is real and has a very human cost, but ISIS made a mistake when it declared war on the world. The world is answering back, and ISIS will be driven from its land, left to languish in cyberspace where it will have to settle for inspiring attacks it has no ability to coordinate. The nations of the world will not stop until their citizens are safe and their lost avenged.

1

A STORIED

TRADITION

America's problems with Muslim hostage-takers began shortly after the end of the Revolutionary War. Mediterranean markets for American wheat, flour, fish, and rice were a critical strength of the fledgling economy, but the ships found themselves in unfriendly waters. Since the days of camel caravans across the Sahara, countries had paid tributes to the local tribes for safe passage. Unprotected goods were seized, and merchants and laborers taken as slaves. Merchant ships to the region were finding some of the same problems on the high seas and in ports along North Africa. As Thomas Jefferson took office in 1801, the conflict was boiling over. America would soon find itself at war against a Muslim nation for the first time.

SHORES OF TRIPOLI

President Jefferson took office facing a difficult problem: The United States had been paying tribute to the nations of Tunisia, Algiers, and Morocco, but it was behind on the bill. In Tripoli, the ruler released a seized American ship as a gesture of good will but sent along a warning: pay the tribute or America will find itself at war. Seven years earlier, Jefferson had addressed the issue in a report to Congress, where he had recommended that the United States escalate the conflict by sending the navy to defend American vessels in the Mediterranean Sea. He told Congress that America had three options: "war, tribute, or ransom."[1] Tribute and ransom had been America's policy since its early efforts at international trade, but the growing power of the US Navy now offered another solution.

The leader of Tripoli settled the matter for Jefferson by declaring war on the United States in 1801. The battles would rage over the next four years. Initially, the war had poor support from Congress and the American people, but Marine Lieutenant Stephen Decatur's daring raid on the *Philadelphia* inspired America to fully commit to the effort. The size of the fleet was increased to eleven ships, and the tide of war began to turn in favor of the Americans.[3] America struck a secret deal with the Tripoli leader's brother, the former pasha Hamet, to help the Americans in exchange for support for his leadership after the war. Under siege on two fronts, the Tripolitan leader Pasha Yusuf Qaramanli was forced to negotiate terms.

In a stunning reversal that would be a hallmark for future Western dealings with partners in the Middle East, the United States opted not to make good on its promise to reinstate the ex-pasha and instead allowed Qaramanli to remain in power. The American prisoners, mostly from the crew of the USS *Philadelphia*, were released after a small ransom payment. America had secured its first victory on foreign soil. While 90 percent of the American hostages were returned, the next 200 years would prove that to be the exception to dealings between the civilized world and those who take hostages in the name of Islam.[4]

A DARING RAID

British admiral Horatio Nelson, hero of the Napoleonic Wars, called it "the most daring act of the age." A navy frigate, the USS *Philadelphia,* responding to continued threats against American vessels and sailors, had been deployed to the Mediterranean Sea by President Thomas Jefferson. The ship was involved in a pitched battle with a pirate ship and gave chase into the harbor. Unfamiliar with the shoals of the coast of modern-day Libya, the ship ran aground on a coral reef and was captured. The entire crew of 315 sailors was taken prisoner, and the wounded ship was towed into the harbor by enemy vessels.[2]

The ship was a marvel for its time and a huge boon to the pirates. The ship could be restored and reflagged as a Tripolitan warship and used as a model to build a new fleet of dangerous ships. American and European vessels braving the North African coast would find themselves facing off against one of the most capable warships of the era. Commodore Edward Preble ordered the ship destroyed before it could become a threat. Lieutenant Stephen Decatur led the raid. He crammed seventy men into a stolen ship designed to hold thirty sailors. Under a false flag, the ship, named *Intrepid,* sailed into the harbor and attacked the *Philadelphia* and its twenty guards. The Tripolitan guards were swiftly overwhelmed and the ship set aflame; there was no loss of American life. As the Americans sailed out of the harbor, the flames reached the powder stores and the ship exploded. Decatur returned home a hero, cementing the legend of the US Marines who still pay homage to the raid in their anthem, which specifically mentions their win on "the shores of Tripoli."

The burning of the USS *Philadelphia* off the coast of Tripoli, in 1804, is portrayed here. The battle between the United States and the Barbary States, as the opponents were known, marked the first war between the United States and a Muslim nation.

BRANCHING OUT

The United States has long held the policy of not negotiating with terrorists who take Americans as hostages, promising prosecution to the fullest extent of the law for hostage-takers.[5] This policy is designed to protect Americans from becoming hostages by removing one of the oldest motivations: ransom for cash. Though recent hostage situations have ended badly, earlier incidents were resolved diplomatically.

On November 4, 1979, the US Embassy in Iran was attacked by a mob of three thousand protestors angry with the Americans for supporting the former shah, who had been deposed by the recent revolution. In total, sixty-six Americans were captured and held hostage. The Iranians demanded the shah be returned to Iran to face charges of human rights violations. They also wanted all of the shah's property declared as stolen from the Iranian people. Finally, they demanded that the United States cease all interference in Iranian politics. The grievance stemmed from a US-supported coup back in the fifties, when the US helped the shah regain control of the government after he lost an election. The Iranians had been angry with America ever since and seized this opportunity make their point.

The United States was outraged and ceased all purchases of Iranian oil. Additionally, Iranian assets worth billions were frozen in US banks. The US and its foreign partners began to apply significant pressure on Iran to release the hostages. The Iranians released thirteen hostages it deemed not to be potential spies, along with an embassy employee who had become ill, but kept fifty-two Americans as hostages until their political demands were met.

Five months into the crisis, and with no end in sight, the US opted for a military raid to retrieve the hostages. It did not go well. Helicopters malfunctioned and one crashed, killing eight US soldiers. The attempt was embarrassing. Finally, Algeria offered to serve as a middleman for negotiations between the two countries. On January 20, 1981, after 444 days, the Americans were released.[7] Though the United States agreed no longer to interfere in Iran and unfreeze its assets in the US, those promises were never fully realized. But the Islamic Republic of Iran had shown the world that the United States could be forced to negotiate.

EVOLUTION OF EVIL

In the chaos of Afghanistan after the Russian invasion, a group of US-backed fighters was gaining strength. After driving out the

MUNICH OLYMPICS

Eight men with duffel bags and tracksuits would not have looked out of place at the Olympic Village in Munich, Germany, in 1972. That is, until they reached their target, donned masks, and began to pull pistols, machine guns, and grenades from the large bags. The men belonged to a group called Black September. They forced their way into the sleeping quarters of the Israeli Olympic team. In the initial struggle, they killed a wrestling coach and a weightlifter, leaving them with nine hostages. The Olympic Village awoke to the grim news of an active hostage crisis in their midst.

The kidnappers wanted 234 Palestinians released from Israeli jails and two German terrorists imprisoned in Germany. They also wanted a plane to Cairo, Egypt. To demonstrate their resolve, the terrorists dumped one of the dead bodies out of a window. German police settled on a plan and readied a plane, whose crew had been replaced with sixteen police officers. The plan fell apart when the Germans on the plane left their posts out of fear. When the terrorists arrived and found the plane empty, a firefight erupted, killing most of the kidnappers and all of the remaining Israeli hostages.[6] It was a new era in the brutal killing of hostages at the hands of politically motivated terrorists.

After 444 days, the hostages held by Iran were released in January 1981. Although the United States has long had a policy that forbids negotiating with terrorists for hostages, Iran showed that the United States could sometimes be forced to the negotiating table.

Russians and supporting the creation of an Islamic government in Afghanistan, the fighters turned their attention outward. The group's leader, Osama bin Laden, named his group al-Qaeda (meaning "the base" in Arabic). The group carried out a series of attacks, ending in the destruction of the twin towers in New York City on September 11, 2001. The attack caused cash-flow problems for the group as US and international agencies began cutting off funding sources to the group. Terrorist groups are nothing if not inventive, and al-Qaeda quickly took to the ancient tradition that hounded merchants of the Sahara centuries before: kidnapping for ransom.

Since 2008, al-Qaeda's largest source of income has been the hundreds of millions it receives in ransom payments from countries around the world.[8] As the group spread around the Middle East, Asia, and Africa, the group's ability to grab and sell hostages improved, especially after the horrific execution of some hostages. In a particularly brutal video, AQI leader Abu Musab al-Zarqawi personally beheaded an American businessman in Iraq. Even al-Qaeda was appalled; it chastised and eventually disowned the group, which later changed its name to ISIS.[9]

ISIS would take al-Qaeda's hostage policy to new extremes. It exploited hostages for far more than money as it waged psychological and political war against its enemies. In the next section we'll look at the most well-known of ISIS's victims, freelance reporter James Foley. His killing would prove a gruesome escalation of ISIS's campaign and one that would draw the ire of the world on the terrorist group.

2

STRANGER IN A

STRANGE LAND

James Foley wanted to make the world a better place. After graduating college, he worked in underprivileged schools in Arizona. Later, he taught classes to high-school dropouts to help them get their GEDs, and then he went on to teach at a prison. Turning his attention to the problems of the world, he became a journalist and found himself in several far-flung locales. Undeterred after a forty-four-day stint as a hostage in Libya, Foley went to Syria to cover the plight of people in Raqqa, the capital of the Islamic State.

In 2012, a few days before Thanksgiving, he was captured by ISIS. For sixteen months there was no word, and his family began to fear the worst. Then, a ray of hope: two Spanish prisoners who had been held with Foley in Syria were released. Foley's family received a ransom email from ISIS demanding $132 million for his release, but US policy was clear—negotiating with terrorists was forbidden. Ransom payments would be a crime.[1] The US policy is based on the idea that such negotiations and payments would encourage the taking of other Americans and create a funding source for terror.

Journalists Tim Hetherington, James Foley, and Chris Hondros (*left to right*) are memorialized at the Bronx Documentary Center in New York. Foley was killed by ISIS militants in 2014.

After receiving intelligence that indicated Foley's location, the US launched a Special Operations Forces raid to recover the journalist, but they were too late. By the time the team arrived on site, Foley had been moved, lost again to the lawless spaces of Syria. In August 2014, Foley's family received one last email from his captors, decrying the US refusal to pay for his release. Time was running out. A few days later, a video was released that showed a British jihadi beheading an orange-clad James Foley after forcing him to read a statement condemning US interference in Muslim lands.

President Barack Obama spoke with the grieving family, telling them that he was heartbroken.[2] Foley had devoted his life to helping the oppressed and abused. He sought to lift others from their plight through telling the world their stories.

Following his beheading, ISIS released a video of James Foley's murder. The death of the Western journalist was used as propaganda material by the terror group, while those in the West were horrified by the brutality.

James Foley was the first American killed by ISIS, but he would not be the last.

KAYLA MUELLER

"Every human being should act. They should stop this violence. People are fleeing. We can't bear this. It's too much. I hope you

can tell the entire world what I have said here, and what I've seen." This heartfelt message was one of the last that American aid worker Kayla Mueller wrote on her blog before being captured.[3] After graduating college in 2009, Mueller devoted her life to the refugees of the world. She worked in India, Israel, and Palestine. She wanted to help those she found in need and write about their plight to inspire others to help. She was captured by ISIS as she left a hospital in Aleppo, Syria.

Mueller had known some of the journalists who had been held and beheaded by the group. After her capture, she was tortured as her tormentors tried to convince her to admit that she was really an American spy. Once they were satisfied that she was indeed a humble aid worker, she was sent to a house that served as a slave market for other women captured by ISIS, mostly from a Christian minority group, the Yazidis. While in captivity, she passed the time exercising and teaching her captors to make origami cranes.

ISIS sent an email to Mueller's family demanding $7 million for her release. Multiple mediation attempts failed. An American military operation to retrieve her found only the empty building where she had been held. It would be months before her fate was known. Kayla Mueller was killed, but her cause of death is uncertain. ISIS claimed that she had been killed in an American airstrike. There was no proof beyond a picture of a destroyed building. Two other women with whom she was held escaped

ORANGE JUMPSUITS

It is a scene that has become all too familiar: hostages in orange jumpsuits are forced to kneel in front of black-clad terrorists to be executed. Videos from all over the world have featured the same pattern, but why? The symbolism stems from one of the most embarrassing failures of discipline in the US Army. In 2003, the US Army took over an old prison in Iraq called Abu Ghraib and repurposed it to hold suspected terrorists arrested in Iraq. Lower enlisted guards with little or no prison operations experience were put in charge of the prisoners. With little outside supervision, conditions in the prison worsened. The prison guards began abusing their inmates.

It might have all gone unnoticed if the pictures had not come out. The photos depicted scenes of depravity and mistreatment of prisoners on an epic scale. Naked men were piled on top of each other or placed in poses that simulated sex acts. One man was placed on a box wearing a pointed hood. He had wires attached to his fingers and genitals. He had been told if he moved he would be electrocuted. There were scenes of prisoners being tortured by snarling dogs. The common element in many of the photos was the bright orange prison jumpsuits worn by many of the prisoners.

The prison staff was fired and charged with mistreatment of prisoners. Officers in charge of the prison were fired or punished. The general charged with investigating the incident described a host of "sadistic, blatant, and wanton criminal abuses."[4] When ISIS dresses its prisoners in orange jumpsuits prior to execution, it is trying to justify its actions as revenge for the abuses at Abu Ghraib.

Kayla Mueller, shown here in 2013, was an aid worker in Syria who was captured and held by ISIS. She was killed in 2015, though it remains disputed whether she was killed by ISIS directly or was a victim of an airstrike by anti-ISIS forces.

and told a different tale about her fate. Abu Bakr al-Baghdadi, the leader of ISIS and the so-called caliph, took Mueller as his unwilling fourth wife.

After months of captivity and enduring frequent rape by Baghdadi, Mueller was reportedly handed off to other less-senior members who wanted her for themselves. A Yazidi slave girl who was held captive by ISIS's second-in-command claims that she was told they killed Mueller because she was American, and America was complicit in the daily bombings by the Syrian government.[5] President Obama found himself expressing his sorrow to yet another American family. He ordered a review of the US policy against negotiating but acknowledged that making such deals would endanger other Americans and finance terrorists.

THEO PADNOS

Theo Padnos spent nearly two years as a hostage in Syria, but he lived to tell the tale. A student of literature and religion, Padnos had spent time in Yemen and Syria. He was interested in how differences between secular and religious Syrians were fueling the conflict there. When he pitched his story idea to several leading newspapers and magazines, the response was less than enthusiastic. Padnos thought that if he were closer to the action he might get a better response. He left for a Turkish town near the Syrian border. He found three men who promised to take him across and connect him with the US-supported rebel forces. After crossing the border, the three men turned on him. Theo Padnos was now a prisoner of one of the many terrorist organizations in Syria.[6]

The group holding Padnos hostage was part of the al-Nusra Front. It shared a parent organization with ISIS and had been claimed as part of the group by ISIS leader Baghdadi. Padnos was moved from prison to prison and constantly encouraged to convert to Islam. His fluency in Arabic led to suspicion about him being a US spy, but his knowledge of the Quran helped to placate his captors.

As tensions escalated between the various jihadist groups in Syria, Padnos found himself accompanying the local al-Nusra leader to another location close to the fighting front. Padnos soon heard that the town they had recently left had been seized

A DANGEROUS PROFESSION

Since the beginning of the campaign against terrorists following the September 11 attacks, more than eight hundred journalists have lost their lives around the world, with four times more deaths in Iraq and Syria than any other country. Thousands more have been arrested by the governments featured in their reporting.[7] Far beyond sitting in a newsroom typing up stories, these brave souls go to some of the most dangerous places in the world to try to expose the plight of those caught in conflict.

Several prominent journalists have been killed by terrorist organizations in horrific fashion. Others have been shot covering fierce battles between rebels and pro-government forces. Still more have been killed by the constant rain of missiles, bombs, and even exploding barrels dropped from helicopters. Additionally, reporters covering crime beats or exposing corruption can become targets of those whom they expose. In dictatorial regimes, reporters can be killed or threatened by the security apparatus of the state, such as the dreaded Mukhabarat in countries like Egypt, Iraq, Jordan, and Syria. Just as often, female reporters are targeted for sexual assault.

In an effort to curb the danger to freelance or self-employed journalists, some newspapers have stopped accepting work from journalists not directly employed or assigned by the paper.[8] The International News Safety Institutes recommends that all journalists have survival training, basic first aid training and equipment, and an understanding of the political and military environment in which they operate.

Journalist Theo Padnos was captured by members of an al-Qaeda offshoot when he snuck into Syria to cover the civil war in 2012. Though he tried to escape several times, he was caught each time before finally being released in 2014.

by ISIS, and many of the remaining fighters executed. Shortly after the execution of James Foley went public, Padnos found himself driven to a UN camp in the Golan Heights area in southwest Syria. Padnos was one of the lucky ones. He was free.

Though America and its citizens are the primary enemies of ISIS, the group is not so picky that it won't take hostages from other countries. After all, many countries are perfectly willing to pay for the return of their citizens, and ISIS knows that an apocalyptic battle will not be cheap.

TAKING ALL
COMERS

Though America and Israel are named as enemies of the Islamic State, the group has not been shy about grabbing hostages from other countries who come to Iraq and Syria. There's a logic to its decision, because other countries have proven willing to pay ransoms for the safe return of their citizens. Expanding its list of offending nations has allowed ISIS to spread its reign of terror while creating a strong source of income for the terrorist organization.

FIRE WITH FIRE

Muath al-Kasasbeh was a striking figure in his flight suit. He was part of an elite group of Jordanian pilots who flew the F-16 Fighting Falcon. Shortly after his marriage, he received orders: his unit would begin participating in the US-led coalition against ISIS. On Christmas Eve 2014, his plane crashed in Syria. After ejecting and landing in a lake, al-Kasasbeh was dragged from the water by armed men. When the pictures

In Amman, Jordan, protestors gathered after ISIS executed a captured Jordanian pilot, Muath al-Kasasbeh. After his plane crashed in Syria, ISIS captured and eventually killed him.

went public, Jordan was publicly outraged but privately began negotiations for his release.

ISIS wasted no time creating propaganda around its captive. He was forced to do an interview with ISIS's magazine, *Dabiq*. In the interview, al-Kasasbeh admitted to participating in the US-led bombing of ISIS weapons on the ground. When asked if he knew what was going to happen to him, he replied that he knew that ISIS would kill him. Then, there emerged a glimmer of hope. ISIS wanted Jordan to release a failed female suicide bomber who was in jail awaiting execution. It offered to trade al-Kasasbeh and a Japanese hostage for the woman.

When ISIS failed to receive an answer from the Jordanian government, it released a video of the execution of the Japanese prisoner. Jordan demanded proof that its pilot was still alive, but its worst fears had been realized. A video appeared online of al-Kasasbeh dressed in the foreboding orange jumpsuit. He was standing in a cage in a soaking-wet jumpsuit. It was not sweat that soaked his clothing—he was soaked in gasoline. ISIS burned the fighter alive and recorded the entire horrible scene, claiming that because the pilot killed with fire, he should be killed with fire.

The king of Jordan was incensed and ordered the immediate execution of the female bomber in custody. Jordan intensified its bombing campaign with fifty-five airstrikes the following day. As the plane returned home, it flew over al-Kasasbeh's village in a salute to its fallen brother. Islamic scholars decried the killing of the pilot, noting that the prophet himself had forbid the killing of anyone with fire.[2] ISIS probably thought that the killing would further divide Jordanians whose support for the Jordanian forces in coalition attacks was mixed, but they miscalculated. Burning the pilot created a martyr and a hero of epic proportions behind

EYE FOR AN EYE

The idea of seeking revenge on someone by inflicting the same damage upon that person that the person caused to you predates Islam by more than two thousand years. In ancient Mesopotamia (modern-day Iraq), a king named Hammurabi had a set of 282 laws inscribed on stone and clay tablets by which to rule his kingdom. The most well-known of the laws was adopted by the tribes of the region and was even used years later in Roman law: "If a man put out the eye of another man, his eye shall be put out."[1]

The Hammurabi Code is one of the earliest instances of written law. The code covers a wide variety of issues, such as slander, trade, slavery, duties of workers, theft, trade, liability, and divorce. The law's prescriptions for offenses vary depending on the social classes of the offender and the offended. Property owners, free men, and slaves were treated differently under the law. For example, Law 218 orders the cutting off of a physician's hands if he kills a free man or property owner through incompetence. The next law, Law 219, requires only monetary payment for the death of a slave from physician error.

Saudi Arabia is one of the few countries that still keep many of the Hammurabi traditions, which allow for public executions for murder and adultery, and maiming in cases of theft. While Saudi Arabia's punishments have drawn condemnation from human rights organizations, ISIS has taken similar measures to horrific extremes. Its reasons are based on its interpretations of the Quran, along with the sayings and behavior attributed to Islam's prophet, Muhammad. One potential way to counter these interpretations is to understand their historical origins and the context within which punishments like these were imposed.

whom the Jordanian people rallied. The king himself swore that his retribution against the group would be relentless.

THE WANDERER

While ISIS usually reserves its condemnation for Western parties, even the Far East has not been immune from its brutality. A Chinese man, Fan Jinghui, was kidnapped by the group in western Iraq. While there are reports that between one hundred and two hundred Chinese citizens (mostly from the Muslim minority group the Uighurs, pronounced WEE-gers) have joined ISIS in its fight in Syria and Iraq, Fan was not there to fight. No one really knows why the self-described professional wanderer went to Iraq. But it would turn out to be a fatal decision.

It's not clear if China knew Fan was in Iraq until he appeared in ISIS's online magazine, *Dabiq*. A full-page ad in the magazine read "Chinese Prisoner for Sale." The ad featured several pictures, as well as biographical information on Fan, with a telegram number for anyone wanting to pay the ransom.[3] ISIS warned that the offer was for a limited time only. China began working behind the scenes to purchase Fan's freedom. In communication with ISIS, China was even able to narrow down Fan's location to the Anbar province in western Iraq. Unfortunately for Fan, no rescue was mounted and no ransom forthcoming.

China lost contact with those holding Fan. Western Iraq is, after all, a war zone. Relentless Russian and French airstrikes broke down the fragile communications network. The limited time offer expired. Fan, along with a Norwegian man who had been featured in the same issue of *Dabiq*, was killed by his ISIS captors.

CHINESE MUSLIMS

Many don't realize that 77 percent of the world's Muslims do not live in the Middle East. There are 1.6 billion Muslims in the world, and only 317 million live in the Middle East and North Africa. One of the least-known Muslim sects is the Uighurs in China. They live in an autonomous region of Xinjiang in western China. This means that they are part of China but allowed to have their own local government. Uighurs are actually of Eurasian descent and have more in common with the Central Asian peoples than their Chinese countrymen in the East.

The richness of natural resources in the region has led to a significant amount of attention from the Chinese government. Despite their autonomy, Uighurs frequently complain that they suffer continuous human rights abuses at the hands of the Chinese state. For example, two hundred people were killed during a protest in 2009.

Several high-profile terrorist attacks in the East have been blamed on the Uighurs, most likely in retaliation for their mistreatment at the hands of the Chinese government. Most notably, the Uighurs are blamed for a knife attack at a train station in China that killed twenty-nine people. At least twenty Uighurs have been arrested in Afghanistan, and more than one hundred have gone to Syria and Iraq to join ISIS. But these numbers must be kept in perspective. There are 10 million Uighurs; very few have directly supported terrorism, despite their disagreements with China and their wish for independence.

Chinese Hui Muslims pray at a holy site, the Imam's Tomb, in Beijing, China, during the Islamic holy month of Ramadan. Although little discussed, there are believed to be more than 20 million Hui Muslims in China.

China has vowed to fight terror in all its forms, but it has largely taken a hands-off approach to the fight in Syria and Iraq. ISIS accused China and Norway of abandoning their citizens.

After the execution, ISIS stepped up its efforts to recruit additional Chinese Muslims to the fight. It even released a song in Mandarin Chinese about the glory of jihad and the duty of every able-bodied Muslim to join the fight. Reports of the execution of Chinese Muslims who had joined ISIS but tried to flee may discourage others from honoring the call to jihad.[4] While ISIS has been sympathetic to the plight of Chinese Muslims, its efforts and attention are more likely to cause an increased crackdown on the Uighurs, and China is likely to continue blaming the Uighurs for nearly every terrorist attack that occurs in the country.

DANIEL RYE OTTOSEN

Daniel Ottosen came to the war like many journalists. He wanted to highlight with his camera the plight of everyday Syrians trying to survive in the midst of chaos. Over the next thirteen months, he would get a closer look than he bargained for. While trying to get permission to use his camera in Syria, he was captured and accused of being a spy. Like most hostages, he was moved from prison to prison. He finally landed in the most dangerous prison. It was the prison where British jihadists had beheaded several of the prisoners.

For months, Ottosen was subjected to various forms of torture. He was hung from a ceiling by his arms. His legs were placed through a tire while his feet were whipped viciously. He considered suicide or converting to Islam to lessen the torture. In the end, he decided to remain true to himself and his fellow prisoners. After thirteen months of captivity, worn ragged from torture and watching his friends disappear one by one, surviving on rare handfuls of olives and bread, Ottosen's family bought his freedom for a little more than $2 million. He remains haunted by his experience. He allowed his ordeal to be captured in a book so that others might know the truth of his captivity.

Pierre Torres (*center*) and Daniel Rye Ottosen (*right*) were held hostage by ISIS along with James Foley. Here, they pose with director Brian Oakes (*left*) at the premiere of a film about Foley.

These three hostages demonstrate just how dangerous it can be for those who cross paths with ISIS. If ISIS can't make money off hostages, it kills them for propaganda value. A troubling trend that we will explore in the next chapter is how ISIS groups are reaching across oceans and taking hostages in incidents around the globe. As the group loses ground in Iraq and Syria, it will likely resort to more foreign actions. It will lash out at innocents abroad as it seeks to maintain revenue streams and continue its campaign of terror.

4

ON FOREIGN

SOIL

ISIS operatives have spread out across the globe. The hostages taken in these attacks are taken as bargaining chips instead of for financial gain. These dangerous situations do not typically end well. ISIS is quick to claim responsibility for the incidents, usually by praising the attackers and warning of other attacks that are sure to come.

HOTEL HORROR

With its tall sweeping walls and pointed arch, the Corinthia Hotel, its palm trees rustling in the ocean breeze, cuts a striking figure against the beach in Tripoli, Libya. The nearby harbor had once been the home of pirates who had troubled the United States enough to get the new nation to launch its first attack on foreign soil back in 1801. The hotel used to be a popular spot for Western businessmen and tourists. The ongoing civil war dried the stream of travelers to a trickle. With its foreign clientele largely absent, the hotel took to renting rooms to local government officials, like Prime Minister Omar al-Hassi. On the morning of January 27, 2015, the morning calm was shattered as a car pulled into the parking lot and exploded. The explosion shattered nearby windows and sent smoke and flame into the cool morning air.

Several armed men poured into the lobby of the hotel, shooting four guards and taking the few residents hostage. Among the hostages was an American businessman, David Berry. Berry was a security contractor working in Libya. Libya's security forces responded to the explosion, trapping the men inside with their hostages. Not known for their patience, the Libyan security forces stormed the hotel. In the fray that followed, ten people were killed and several were injured. One of the attackers was captured and claimed the attack for ISIS as revenge for the death of a Libyan terrorist in American custody. David Berry was among the dead, another American victim of ISIS's campaign of terror.[1]

MADNESS AT THE MUSEUM

The Bardo Museum in Tunisia is a popular spot with tourists and academics who come to look at floor and wall mosaics that predate the palace in which they hang by 1,500–2,000 years. The morning of March 18, 2015, began like any other day. Busloads of tourists, shuttled in from their various cruise ships, arrived to take in the ancient wonders and the beautiful palace that held them. That morning would see around two hundred tourists arrive at the museum. Around noon, the museum's security guards took a coffee break, leaving their charges unprotected. As if on cue, terrorists swarmed the entryway of the museum, gunning down tourists out front. Panicked, many of the remaining tourists fled into the shelter of the fifteenth-century palace. Their attackers followed them inside. The terrorists had machine guns and casually tossed grenades into side rooms as they walked into the museum.

In January 2015, gunmen who claimed to be part of ISIS stormed into the Corinthia Hotel in Tripoli, Libya, killing at least nine people before blowing themselves up. This image shows the immediate aftermath of the attack.

As police arrived on the scene, a siege developed. An unknown number of hostages were being held by an equally unknown number of terrorists. The front of the museum was a horror show of flashing lights and bleeding tourists. Police began to plan their assault to rescue the remaining hostages. Three hours ticked slowly by. Some tourists had been separated from their friends and families. They crouched outside wondering if

their loved ones were still alive inside the museum. After three hours, the Tunisian police had had enough. They breached the doors and windows of the museum and went in with guns blazing. Two of the terrorists died in that assault, while a third escaped. As police began to assess the human toll, they found nineteen dead among the hostages.[2] A plaque on the wall of the museum now memorializes those lost to ISIS that fateful day.

CONCERT CRISIS

Friday the thirteenth, in November 2015, would live up to its benighted reputation for the people of Paris, France, leaving 130 dead and hundreds wounded. The chaos began shortly after nine o'clock that night, as multiple groups attacked at several locations around the City of Love. Most attacks began with a suicide bombing, which was followed up by gunfire from automatic machine guns. Two large-scale attacks were carried out at a soccer stadium and a rock concert. Among the attackers were two men who had traveled to Europe as refugees, seeking asylum from ISIS. Paris was now under attack from at least two men to whom it had opened its arms in kindness.[3]

Unaware of the chaos around the city, the Eagles of Death Metal, a rock band from California, were playing to a packed house at Paris's Bataclan Theater. The theater was full of fans as the band transitioned into one of its signature songs,

Rescuers are seen helping a victim of the November 2015 shooting at the Bataclan Theater in Paris, France. The attack was later attributed to ISIS supporters.

"Kiss the Devil." Suddenly, three gunmen burst through the front door firing machine guns and shouting, "Allahu Akbar" ("God is great"). They mowed down eighty-nine people in their initial assault. The staccato taps of gunfire initially blended in with the music, but as the music abruptly stopped, the death beat continued. The theater exploded into chaos as people pushed for the exits. The terrorists managed to corner eleven people, holding them hostage against the police response that was developing outside. As police worked their way toward the hostages, one of the attackers was shot and detonated a suicide belt.

Arnaud, a forty-one-year-old artist, and his wife had gone to the concert. They found themselves trapped with the two remaining terrorists on a balcony. French police forced their way deeper into the theater, tossing stun grenades as they advanced. In the gunfire that followed, one of the two remaining terrorists

WOLVES IN SHEEP'S CLOTHING?

Since 2005, the number of refugees and displaced persons from the conflicts in the Middle East quintupled from 5 to 25 million people, with nearly half of those from Iraq and Syria.[4] Many of these refugees have flooded Europe and America with dreams of safety, stability, and opportunity. But some among their number have darker dreams—dreams of revenge, killing, and jihad. Authorities found fake Syrian passports at the scenes of various attacks, stirring fears that it was dangerous to welcome refugees from the latest crises.

The real numbers are a little more comforting. Of the 784,000 refugees whom the United States has resettled since 2001, three have been accused of terrorist plots.[5] The low threat is due to the 18–24-month vetting process to which the United States submits potential refugees. Unfortunately for Europe, the problem is more pressing. Masses of people gather in camps along borders in and around Europe. Without reliable vetting methods, and with the dubious nature of paper records in the war-torn Middle East, some terrorists have slipped in with the suffering masses to wreak havoc.

Although the Eagles of Death Metal had their November 2015 concert interrupted by gunfire when ISIS attacked concertgoers at the Paris show, the group returned to the City of Lights in February 2016 to play a free concert and show their support for their French fans.

detonated his belt and the other was shot dead. Arnaud, his wife, and the remaining hostages were saved from the fate of the eighty-nine who lay dead below them. But they did not escape unscathed: Arnaud's eardrum was burst in the suicide belt explosion that left shrapnel embedded in his back.

It was the worst attack on French soil since World War II.[6] The visible reminders have been swept clean, but there are scars—physical and emotional—that endure.

The next year, the Eagles of Death Metal returned to the venue to play another concert. They played and sang, defiant of the terror that would see them silenced.

CHURCH CHAOS

St. Etienne Church is a beautiful building. Its gray roof, perched on ancient stone walls, stands in stark contrast to the brilliant blue skies of Normandy, France. The pale pink lilies and purple lilacs that grow wild in Normandy's verdant fields and ponds scent the summer breezes in July, much as they would have when King Henry the Fifth came across from England to attack France. But the attackers on July 26, 2016, were not foreign invaders. Rather, they were frustrated citizens who had made repeated attempts to go to Syria to join ISIS but had been turned back at the Turkish border. Inspired by ISIS's war against the West and Christianity, they settled on a target closer to home: a local Catholic church.

Mass was underway at the small church. It was sparsely attended, being a Tuesday morning. Father Jacques Hamel was in the midst of his sermon to two parishioners and two nuns when the door to the small church swung open. Two men rushed into the church shouting, "Allahu Akbar." At least one of the men had been known to police after his attempts to go to Syria to join ISIS. That morning, he was still wearing his ankle

HOLY WAR

ISIS has tried very hard to frame its conflict as a continuation of the ancient battles between Muslims and Christians during the Crusades. In 1095, Pope Urban II of the Latin Church encouraged fighters to go help the Byzantine emperor and liberate Jerusalem. In exchange for their service, fighters were promised salvation. They were given a guarantee of heaven and forgiveness of any previous sins or sins committed in service to the church. The papal decree set off 200 years of wars. During the wars, the holy city changed hands numerous times.

One of the reasons ISIS likes the story of the Crusades is that the Christian invaders were eventually driven out. Jerusalem remained in the control of Muslims for the next 900 years. The Christians lost, and it is a reminder ISIS wants to communicate to what it considers the modern-day equivalent of Rome, the United States.[7] Despite the flaws in the analogy, it is a powerful message, as evidenced by the thousands who have flocked to fight in the modern jihad.

tracker, a condition of his parole. When the jihadists tried to force the eighty-four-year-old priest to kneel, he resisted. They slit his throat, killing the beloved priest. Then the pair turned their attention to one of the parishioners and attacked him with their knives. In the chaos that ensued, one of the nuns managed to escape and notify police. As the police surrounded the church, the two men rounded up the hostages and began to plan their escape. Realizing that no escape would be possible, the two men rushed outside into a hail of police gunfire; both were killed.

In July 2016, ISIS supporters attacked a church in Normandy, France, killing the local priest. Citizens are shown here laying flowers and lighting candles outside the town's city hall to memorialize the victim.

ISIS claimed the attack as yet another in their campaign against Western churches.[8]

It is clear that ISIS refuses to be limited to its small, dusty corner of the world. In the next section, we will look at those caught in ISIS-held lands. The brutal treatment and oppression they have experienced further demonstrates the lengths to which ISIS will go to seize and maintain power.

CITIES UNDER

SIEGE

Foreigners in ISIS lands and abroad are not the ones who suffer at the hands of ISIS. As the terrorist group has seized territory in Iraq and Syria, the innocents caught in its path have faced unimaginable horrors. Religious minority groups have been rounded up and sold into slavery or killed. Entire cities have found themselves under the thumb of a medieval code of laws and religious prescriptions enforced under threat of death.

TERROR ON THE MOUNTAIN

The mountains of northern Iraq are the home to a small religious group that very few in the world even knew existed before ISIS threatened to exterminate them. The Yazidis are frequently referred to as Christian in the Western media, but that label is not accurate. Yazidis believe that an angel was cast out of heaven for arguing with God about the fate of man. This angel, Malek Taus, takes the form of a peacock and now serves on Earth as a mediator between man and God. Unfortunately for the Yazidis, the idea of an angel who was cast out of heaven

In 2014, Yazidi men and women in Hanover, Germany, protested the attacks against the Yazidi people in Iraq. Since ISIS's formation, they have heavily targeted the Yazidi population.

for disagreeing with God about the fate of man exists in most of the world's major religions. Those religions refer to this angel by a different name: Satan. Due to this perception of the Yazidis as devil-worshippers, they have been persecuted for centuries.

When the Islamic State swept through northern Iraq, the Yazidis were forced to flee. Those who were unable to flee found themselves prisoners of ISIS. Declared infidels by decree of ISIS, the Yazidis had none of the protections prescribed in the Quran and Hadith for other monotheistic religious groups, like the Christians and Jews. Older men and women were separated and left to die in the desert. Young men of fighting age were killed. Boys too young to fight were taken to schools to become the next generation of ISIS fighters, the cubs of ISIS. Women were taken to markets and sold, or given as rewards to ISIS fighters and commanders.

The Yazidis who escaped from ISIS made their way to Mount Sinjar in northern Iraq. Approximately 50,000 Yazidis found themselves trapped on the mountain with no food, water, or medicine.[2] ISIS fighters were heading toward the mountain. When the world learned of the Yazidis' plight, it responded generously. Air drops of supplies began to rain down on the besieged mountain. Less pleasant packages, in the form of precision bombs and missiles, fell on the ISIS attackers. The Kurdish military of northern Iraq began airlifting the stranded

A GIRL'S JOURNEY

Narin (an assumed name to protect the girl and her family) was fourteen years old when she and her family heard the bad news: ISIS was coming toward their small village. The family grabbed what they could and fled, but they were captured by the Islamic State. As Narin and the other women were taken away, they heard the gunshots that ended the lives of all the young adult males from her village. There were times ahead that would lead Narin to wonder whether the men got the better end of the deal.

Narin was taken to an abandoned school building that was filled with other women who had been kidnapped by ISIS fighters. The women were urged to convert to Islam, but most refused. For nearly three weeks, the women were kept in a small room. Once a day they were fed and told to convert. Each day they refused, despite the cursing of their guards. Eventually, some of the women were given to ISIS commanders as concubines. Islamic tradition allows for infidels captured during war to be kept as slaves. Narin was beaten daily by her captor, who repeatedly tried to rape her.

When her captor was away at prayer one evening, Narin used a kitchen knife to break the lock that held her captive. Disguised under a heavy *niqab* (a full-body covering that leaves only the eyes exposed), she fled the school and met up with a friend who drove her away from her prison. Over the next several days, Narin hid under the niqab as she made her way north, first by car and then by plane. She was eventually reunited with her family, who had found themselves trapped on Mount Sinjar.

Narin is safe, but every day she thinks of the others who were taken with her. Many of those women are still slaves of ISIS.[1]

Yazidis to safety. But not all of the Yazidi community has been so fortunate. Several thousand Yazidis have been killed or captured by the Islamic State, and 500,000 have been driven from their homes and villages, fleeing from ISIS.[3]

THE FALL OF MOSUL

It is a surreal scene: An ISIS fighter in uniform with an AK-47 machine gun strapped across his chest, surrounded by children, pushes a child in a wheelchair around a brightly colored theme park. The rides are in motion and the children are smiling. A British reporter took to the internet to talk about how nice everything was in the city. But beneath the veneer, and out of sight of the cameras, are the billboards. They warn women to cover their faces and bodies and not wear perfume under threat of punishment—or death. The local hotel has had its beautiful carvings scraped off and ISIS flags raised above it.[4] Mosul belongs to ISIS, and the Iraqi troops charged with its safekeeping have melted into the desert.

The people of Mosul have been subjected to ISIS's interpretations of a legal code that is nearly 1,500 years old. A mish-mash of Quranic verses, statements reportedly issued by the prophet Muhammad (Hadith), and even reports of varying repute that describe things that people saw the prophet do (Sunna) are used as references. In Mosul, this means that women must cover themselves from head to foot. They even have to wear gloves to avoid showing any of their skin and causing the men to feel temptation. Even smoking is forbidden in ISIS territory. Giant bonfires of cigarettes have been featured in ISIS videos.

In a strange twist, ISIS has taken up the administrative duties of managing the city. It runs schools and courts, and even collects the garbage in front of houses. It charges the residents of the city a 25 percent tax on all income to support

A member of the Islamic State carries the black flag of ISIS down the street in Raqqa, Syria. Because of the ongoing civil war in Syria, the country has been especially vulnerable to ISIS.

the government. Christians and Jews must pay an additional tax called the *jizya,* as payment for the protection they receive at the hands of their Muslim overlords. School is in session, but the subjects and teaching materials are horrifying. Children are indoctrinated into ISIS's twisted view of Islam and taught that death as a martyr is the most glorious of career paths. The twisted curriculum has led some parents to withdraw their children, preferring no education to ISIS's teachings.[6]

CAPITAL OF ISIS

Before the Islamic State, Raqqa, Syria, was a cosmopolitan city. Though primarily Muslims, the residents were largely left to their own devices. One could do or wear (or even smoke) anything they wanted.[7] Now the city, declared the capital of the Islamic State, is beset by jihadist checkpoints. Stonings and even beheadings are weekly occurrences for those who run afoul of their brutal captors. Thousands of normal Syrians who have no loyalty to ISIS find themselves trapped in the city with little work and under the constant surveillance of Islamic police forces. Even women find themselves stopped and searched by female jihadists charged with maintaining piety.

Frequent bombings from every side of the conflict have left residents without water, electricity, and many other necessities. Those wanting to work must swear allegiance to ISIS, who rules over the town through a series of increasingly bizarre edicts on behavior and dress. The situation is untenable, but there is hope. A coalition of forces from around the world is working its way toward the trapped residents of Raqqa.

In the next section, we'll explore the justification ISIS uses for its treatment of hostages, many of whom they consider prisoners of war. It takes a twisted interpretation of the scriptures of Islam to justify its behavior. ISIS believes it is acting

MAKING AN ARMY

The Iraqi army's stunning collapse in the face of ISIS called into serious question the US efforts to train and equip the fledgling force. In 2003, when the US swept into Baghdad after toppling Iraqi dictator Saddam Hussein, one of its first acts was to disband the Iraqi army. While US forces provided interim security, the United States hurriedly assembled an Iraqi force to take over for them. But after spending more than ten years and $25 billion to assemble the new Iraqi army, the United States has failed to create an effective fighting force for the country, despite continuous claims of progress and success by US military officials.[5]

One of the challenges is demographic. Most Iraqis are Shia, but the Sunnis have dominated the government and military for decades. As the ranks filled with Shia soldiers, there were reports in Sunni areas of atrocities committed as revenge for years of oppression by their Sunni countrymen. The Kurds in the north have been the most effective military force, but there are decades of mistreatment at the hands of Saddam Hussein's government that make any integration with Iraqi forces difficult.

The latest efforts seem to be more effective, as a coalition of military groups are working together to liberate the city of Mosul, once abandoned by Iraqi forces. Shia militias, in coordination with Kurdish fighters and Sunni guard forces, have been working toward reclaiming their country from ISIS.

If the last fifteen years have proven anything, it is that an outside power cannot just walk into another country and create a cohesive and effective military in that country through sheer will and financing.

After announcing their caliphate in 2014, ISIS held a military parade in Syria, showing off their power for locals and later releasing images from the parade to taunt the world.

according to God's will, and though Muslim scholars frequently point out the inaccuracies of ISIS interpretations, their message hasn't stopped thousands from declaring allegiance to the group and accepting its interpretations of these ancient scriptures.

6

INTERPRETING
GOD'S WILL

There is constant argument over whether the Islamic State represents Islam. It certainly believes that it does, but more than a billion Muslims refuse to acknowledge the group or its right to interpret and impose Islamic law on the world. ISIS believes it is charged with establishing a global society dominated by Muslims where all live according to God's word, but who speaks for God? For ISIS, it is a hodge-podge of sources and some questionable interpretations.

GOD'S LAW

As Islam evolved in the seventh century, its founder, Muhammad, found himself responsible for thousands of people. As the governor in Medina, he had to answer questions about the law. As a general in charge of troops and battles, he had to answer questions about the reasons for and conduct in war. Once Muhammad was gone, all people had left to help them answer new questions were the verses that Muhammad had recited from the Quran, his advice (Hadith), and records of his behavior (Sunna). None of these were written down until years later. When they were finally transcribed, there was disagreement about which sayings or behavior could be attributed to the prophet.

Over the years, several schools of thought developed as to which interpretations were correct and which scriptures were

STRONG AND WEAK

Muhammad is the ultimate authority in Islam. He was the source of the Quran, and his life is the source of most of the traditions we associate with the faith today. As such, anything he said or did represents the perfect example of behavior for any devout Muslim. For hundreds of years, people spread these stories. Along the way, clever people inserted their own sayings and stories to justify their positions in arguments or impose their will on others. As the stories and sayings were collected into books, scholars were left with a difficult problem: how could they know which words and acts were truly those of the Prophet?

Early scholars decided on a system of attribution called *isnad*. This attribution is akin to saying, "My mother said that your mother heard from her brother that his neighbor said that the priest overheard Muhammad say this quote." Certain chains are considered stronger than others, however, leading to a classification system. Hadith that are considered true and actionable with a strong chain of attribution are called *sahih* ("correct" in Arabic). Weaker attributions were labeled as *hasan* (good) or *da'if* (weak). Many of the scriptures to which ISIS refers fall into the "weak" category, and some of its treatment of prisoners is outright forbidden in sahih or correct Hadith.[1]

Pakistani Muslim women read the Quran while wearing niqabs, or full head coverings. While viewed as conservative to the West, these women would be underdressed according to ISIS rule, which prefers women wear full-face burqas instead.

most important. Modern jihadists subscribe to a strict, violent interpretation, called Wahhabism, that arose in Saudi Arabia. Wahhabism believes that the prophet and those around him, his rightly guided companions, set the example for perfect living. Some go so far as to model their appearance on descriptions of the prophet, keeping their hair and mustache short while wearing a long beard and pants that end just above the ankles.

Wahhabis are the spiritual successors of a group called the Kharijites.[2] After Muhammad's death, there were disagreements about succession and some outright battles. During one of these battles, Ali, Muhammad's son-in-law and the leader of Islam at the time, agreed to negotiation after his enemy raised a copy of the Quran on a spear. A group of Ali's soldiers were incensed and abandoned him, forming their own group called the Khawarij ("those that leave" in Arabic), or Kharijites. The Kharijites decided that they could declare whether someone was a true Muslim. It was a dangerous innovation because now the protections and prohibitions against killing Muslims could be lifted by the declaration of one's enemy as a *kafir*, or infidel. The process of calling someone an infidel is called *takfir*. Ali was the first to be killed under this new idea that Muslims could kill other Muslims they deemed unworthy.

Modern jihadists subscribe to these same dangerous ideas. They believe all life and custom should proceed as they did in the seventh century, during the time of Muhammad. They believe that they can determine who is and is not a good Muslim. Since Islam was at war from very early in its existence—and for 1,000 years afterward—there are plenty of examples of conduct in war and the treatment of prisoners and slaves in the religion's texts.

PUNISHING THE INFIDEL

The early years of Islam were incredibly violent and bloody, as Muhammad and his successors spread the faith over half the world. The largest of the caliphates stretched from Spain

An Iraqi federal police officer uses a helmet on a stick to try to draw fire from ISIS fighters. If ISIS fires first, he can pinpoint their location based on the direction of the shooting, giving him a better shot of hitting his target when he fires back.

THREAT OF ISLAM

Muhammad's new religion threatened the status quo in the lands that we today call Saudi Arabia. Wars broke out between the tribes that supported the new religion and those who felt threatened by it. Mecca was a major pilgrimage site for many religions, and its central square, the Kaaba, held many idols of various faiths. Each year thousands of people flocked to the city and its markets. This meant lots of money for the shop owners and the tribe that controlled the Kaaba. Muhammad's declaration that there was no god but God endangered a crucial source of income for the ruling tribe, the Quraysh.

If all the idols in the Kaaba were false, then there would be no reason to make a pilgrimage and spend money in the surrounding markets. Muhammad was a direct threat to the financial well-being of the Quraysh. As such they tried multiple times to have him killed. Eventually they drove him out of Mecca to Medina. This flight to Medina is so significant that it marks the first year of the modern Islamic, or *hijri*, calendar.

From Medina, Muhammad would raise an army that would return to Mecca and reclaim the city of his birth. One of Muhammad's first acts was to destroy every idol in the Kaaba, consistent with his declaration. Reports vary, but of the 360 idols in the Kaaba, Muhammad destroyed everything except for a painting of Mary with Jesus and another of the prophet Abraham.[6] It turns out the ruling tribe had been worried for nothing, as Muhammad declared pilgrimage to the Kaaba as a religious duty for every Muslim. This would lead to the giant crowds that circle the cloth-draped cube in the heart of Mecca every year, even today.

to eastern Asia before it was mostly beaten back to the Middle East in the fifteenth century. The level of violence required Muhammad to establish rules for conduct. He called his wars part of the jihad, or holy struggle, but noted that once the war was over, the real jihad was man's struggle to obey the word of God.[3]

One of Muhammad's first declarations about war significantly improved the outlook for prisoners taken in war. Muhammad said that anyone who takes a prisoner is responsible for that person's well being, for clothing and feeding the prisoner.[4] While all of the major schools of Islamic law validate the killing of enemies in combat, or male prisoners afterward, there are many examples of Muhammad pardoning, ransoming, or sentencing literate prisoners to teach Muslims to read and write as a punishment instead of death.[5]

The killing of Jordanian pilot Muath al-Kasasbeh highlights how ISIS has twisted the scriptures to justify something that was expressly forbidden by the prophet himself. Muhammad said that no man should kill with fire because killing by fire was reserved for God.[7] Yet ISIS burned the pilot alive, in a cage, in direct contradiction of this prohibition. Its reason lies in a concept called *qisas*, found in chapter 16, verse 126, of the Quran, which states, "And if you punish them, punish with an equivalent of that with which you were harmed." By ISIS logic, this verse trumps anything Muhammad might have said, because the Quran is the ultimate source of law. This verse justifies the idea of an eye for an eye first established in the ancient code of Hammurabi. Since pilots drop bombs and kill with fire, then ISIS claims it is justified in killing the pilot with fire despite the prophet's prohibition. Its deadly interpretations, coupled with its belief that it can declare someone unfaithful and kill that person, puts all the world's people, even Muslims, in danger.

Haifa is a thirty-six-year-old Iraqi Yazidi woman who was kidnapped and made to be a sex slave by ISIS. Haifa and her younger sister were among thousands of Yazidi women captured by ISIS in 2014.

PEOPLE IN CHAINS

The enslavement of those conquered in war is a practice as old as war itself. Islam altered the landscape by prohibiting the taking of other Muslims or any of the protected people (Christians and Jews) as slaves.[8] ISIS, however, has proven willing to ignore such restrictions. Unfortunately for the Yazidis in northern Iraq, they are not considered protected people. Thousands of Yazidis have been kidnapped and enslaved to serve as wives or unpaid prostitutes using a practice called temporary marriage.

ISIS believes that the restoration of slavery is part of a prophecy that will bring about Armageddon and a global Islamic State.[9] Once again, ISIS is ignoring a strong Hadith in which the prophet forbade the taking as a slave any free person. ISIS instead points to the history of Islamic battles where the prophet himself took and kept slaves. ISIS believes that modern life should be lived according to the example of a man who lived nearly 1,500 years ago, and slavery was a common practice then.

It is clear that ISIS will continue to justify its treatment of hostages and its taking of slaves using the Quran, Hadith, and Sunna. Despite disagreements from most Muslim scholars, the group believes that it has the right to interpret the scriptures any way that it wants in order to justify what it wants to do.

Countries around the world have to deal with their citizens being captured by ISIS. While some countries refuse to negotiate, others are willing to pay dearly for the release of their citizens. In the next section, we'll look at some of these ransom cases and the lengths to which countries will go to recover their citizens, even if it may encourage the kidnapping of others.

7

FREE

AT LAST

It is a terrible conundrum. If a loved one is kidnapped by a terrorist group like ISIS, there are two choices: not pay and the loved one dies, or pay and help the group kill and kidnap others. For a parent, it must be a terrible choice. A parent wants to protect their child no matter what the consequence. For hundreds of families each year, it is a choice that must be made. To pay or not to pay, that is the question. There is no easy answer.

THE PRICE OF LIFE

Ransoming prisoners is a practice as old as war itself. Whether the ransom involves money, resources, or a trade for another life, it is a lucrative trade. Al-Qaeda, the group from which ISIS developed, has earned hundreds of millions of dollars since 2008 through kidnappings, and the price is going up. In 2003, a hostage could be ransomed for $200,000. Today, demands start at $10 million and only go up from there. It's become such a big business that some criminal organizations work on commission.

Japanese prime minister Shinzo Abe condemned ISIS's execution of a Jordanian pilot, as well as their murders of two Japanese hostages only days earlier.

THE INTERMEDIARY

Qatar has spent much of the conflict against ISIS in a gray area. While accusations have been levied against the nation as a financer of the group,[1] it has also been the primary negotiator through which European countries have successfully retrieved their citizens. Qatar has openly supported groups like Hamas, a Palestinian group that has been designated a terrorist organization by the United States and most of Europe. Yet, the parents of Kayla Mueller, an American kidnapped by ISIS, have said that Qatar was far more helpful in attempting to free their daughter than the US government.[2] When the United States wanted to negotiate for the release of Bowe Bergdahl, an American who left his base in Afghanistan and had been captured, they called Qatar.

Ghanim Khalifa al-Kubaisi is the director of intelligence services for Qatar. He has been instrumental in negotiating for the release of several hostages, though he denies any outright payments of ransom money.[3] Kubaisi has sent operatives deep into Syria to negotiate with groups like al-Nusra Front, an ISIS affiliate. In chapter 2, we met Theo Padnos, for whom terrorists had demanded amounts up to $125 million. With Qatar's intervention on his behalf, Padnos was freed with no money paid.

They take hostages and give them to the terrorist groups in exchange for a portion of the profits.[4]

Dozens of European hostages have been released for ransom.[5] England is one of the few countries that conforms with the US policy of not negotiating with terrorists. The policy has led to uncomfortable situations for the country; in some hostage situations, British captives were killed while other Europeans were released to their families.

It comes down to a question of the value of human life—a question for which there is no simple answer. If a family pays for the release of their loved one and thereby facilitates terrorist activities that kill or kidnap others, do they share some of the blame for the future activity for having enabled it? Can the family be held responsible for what the group does with the money when they have no say in the activities of the group?

Terrorists know who pays and who does not. Jean-Paul Rouiller, the director of the Geneva Center for Training and Analysis of Terrorism, believes that the terrorists are now targeting Europeans. The logic is simple: they can make more money off of them. Rouiller points to the statistics that demonstrate more than a third of the hostages taken in recent years are French.[6] His argument may be a bit of a non sequitur, though, since Europeans may simply be more likely to be tourists in North Africa and the Middle East due to the regions' proximity to European countries compared to America. Despite the moral gray area, the results are clear. Dozens of European lives have been saved because their governments, often working through intermediaries, are willing to pay ransoms for the safe return of their citizens.

DARING RAIDS

The United States takes a very different stance from most of the world. America does not negotiate with terrorists. If the

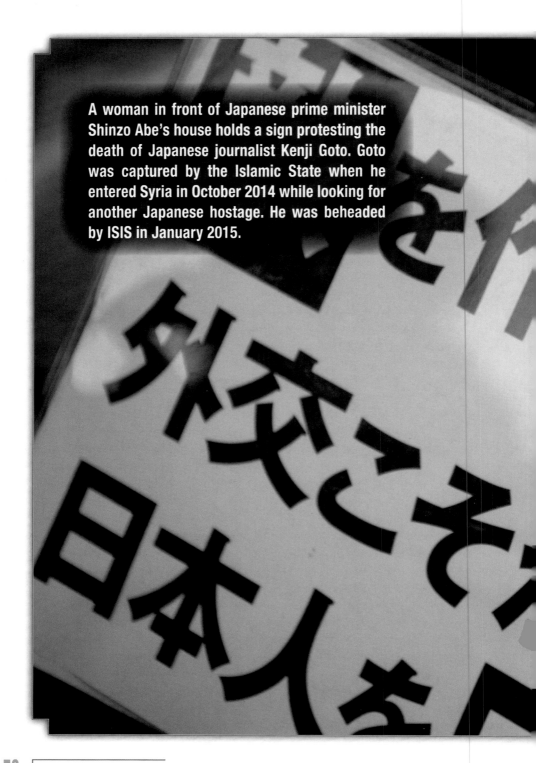

A woman in front of Japanese prime minister Shinzo Abe's house holds a sign protesting the death of Japanese journalist Kenji Goto. Goto was captured by the Islamic State when he entered Syria in October 2014 while looking for another Japanese hostage. He was beheaded by ISIS in January 2015.

AN EXCEPTION?

Despite the United States' official stance that it does not negotiate with terrorists, a recent case seems to directly contradict that position. Bowe Bergdahl, then twenty-three years old, was an army private. In the middle of the night in Afghanistan, Bergdahl left a note on his bed and snuck out into the surrounding wilderness. Whatever his reasons, he was soon captured and held by the Taliban. For five years, Bergdahl's family saw him only in sporadic YouTube videos begging for rescue. Back home, the debate raged: was Bergdahl a prisoner of war or a deserter? Israel had once traded 1,027 Palestinian prisoners for a single Israeli corporal.[7] What was Bergdahl worth to America?

Contentious negotiations ensued. Hardliners in the US government were holding the line: no negotiations. Yet the Taliban had offered to release Bergdahl in exchange for five Taliban prisoners being held in the American prison in Guantánamo Bay, Cuba. The five prisoners were senior Taliban commanders who had been captured on the battlefields of Afghanistan. American leaders were worried that, if released, the men would return to the battlefield and continue their campaign against American forces.

In the end, a compromise was struck with the help of Qatar. The United States would trade the five prisoners for Bowe Bergdahl on the condition that the prisoners, once freed, could not leave Qatar. It ensured the men could not return immediately to the battlefield, but at a cost to American credibility. Despite the hardline stance, the United States had just negotiated with terrorists. It traded five hardened war criminals for one wayward private. Bowe Bergdahl is now standing trial for his desertion and faces accusations that other soldiers died while looking for him.

terrorists will not release American hostages, they can count on a visit from American Special Operations Forces like the Navy SEALs or Army Green Berets. These raids are not without risks to the service members or the hostages, and they have had mixed results since interdiction efforts became prominent in the seventies.

One such rescue began with an urgent phone call in October 2015. Kurdish forces in northern Iraq had received word of twenty hostages being held in a prison near Erbil, Iraq. The prisoners were to be executed after morning prayers the following day. Eleven had been executed at the prison the day before. Their bodies hung from the bridge outside the building. There was no indication that any of the hostages were American, but US Special Operations Forces swung into action. They hastily coordinated a daring helicopter raid on the prison with support from distant artillery. It would be the first time that US forces clashed directly with ISIS.

Delta Force, the elite US Army counterterrorism unit, rode into battle with Kurdish fighters on five helicopters. An airstrike destroyed the cruelly decorated bridge leading to the prison and prevented ISIS from calling in reinforcements. The Kurds began the main assault, but after they became pinned down by enemy fire, US troops sprang into action. They lay down suppressive fire while moving toward their pinned-down partners. An American elite warrior was killed in the gunfight that left twenty ISIS fighters dead and another five captured. The hastily assembled coalition of American and Kurdish fighters reached the prison and were stunned by what they found. There were not twenty hostages in the facility—sixty-nine hostages were crammed into the makeshift prison.[8] The prisoners were a mix of Iraqi Security Forces, local civilians, and even ISIS fighters who had run afoul of their fellow terrorists.

Kurdish Peshmerga soldiers are shown during combat training in Iraq in 2015. The Kurdish forces have been leading the ground war against ISIS in Iraq. Peshmerga soldiers are frequently on the front lines of the battle, and both male and female soldiers have gone up against ISIS during the ongoing war.

As the American and Kurdish forces lifted off with the rescued hostages, an American bomber streaked across the sky. A bright plume flared from the belly of the F-15 fighter. The prison below disintegrated in a hail of steel and fire. It would not hold prisoners, American or otherwise, ever again.

Not every raid has been as successful, and the costs were steep in the lives of the soldiers lost, but that night nearly seventy hostages were spared the death that awaited with the rising sun.

RANSOMING RELIGION

What happens when hostages are taken because of their religion? They belong to no outside nation with which the terrorists can negotiate. Such was the dilemma for 230 hostages seized by ISIS in northern Syria. The terrorist group had seized an entire village of Assyrian Christians, but they were all Syrians, and Syria certainly wasn't going to pay for their release. As Christians, they were in danger of being executed despite Quranic prohibitions against killing "people of the book."9 ISIS wanted $100,000 per hostage.

The call for help went out to the Christians of the world. Secret negotiations ensued with an offer of $5,000 per hostage, which ISIS rejected. The final sum is unknown, but a deal was reached. All 230 hostages were released by ISIS after the global campaign by Christians, Assyrian and otherwise, to raise the funds to free their brothers and sisters. Generally, however, Christians are not a reliable source of income for ISIS. More than 200,000 Syrian Christians have fled their war-torn nation, and in neighboring Lebanon and Iraq, Christian populations have shrunk to less than half of their pre-war levels.[10]

It is clear that ISIS views hostage taking as a useful tool both financially and as propaganda for the so-called caliphate. In the next section, we'll look at how ISIS uses those unfortunate enough to become hostages for its devious ends. As long as ISIS holds lands in Iraq and Syria, Westerners and locals will be subjected to the daily threat of capture and exploitation or death at the hands of the terrorist group. As hostage sources dry up, ISIS will find itself deprived of a significant source of income and political capital.

8

STRATEGY OF

FEAR

ISIS does not just take hostages for the sake of taking them. There is a calculus to its brutality. There is a method to its madness. While hostages have been very profitable for terrorist groups, ISIS has taken the practice to new and gruesome extremes for strategic purposes. Its campaign of fear serves as a powerful recruitment tool, a fear generator, and a dagger in the heart of the tourism industry upon which many countries rely.

RECRUITMENT

ISIS's campaign of terror has centered on spectacular attacks and hostage executions. From the very first execution, ISIS has found a hungry worldwide audience. This audience revels in the violence and killing in ISIS videos and longs to be a part of the action. The recruits attracted by these horrific videos envision themselves as the black-clad terrorists in the film clips, proclaiming their faith in God while killing those they deem less holy.

Captured by ISIS in June 2014, the Turkish hostages shown exiting the plane were released in September 2014. They were greeted by exuberant family members upon their arrival at the airport in Ankara, Turkey, after their release.

Many of the videos feature English speakers, in an attempt to reach a wider audience in the West. These executions, coupled with videos about how great life is under the caliphate, have proven a powerful draw. Some reports show as many as 20,000 recruits from ninety different countries have come to join ISIS, including more than 3,000 hopeful jihadists from Western nations.[2] For every person that goes to Syria to fight, there are countless other supporters who disseminate the videos or encourage others to go and fight. What kind of person is drawn to such horror?

One of ISIS's constant complaints is that Muslims are under attack around the world. For them, the executions of ISIS hostages are revenge for such mistreatment. This revenge motif

STAGED EXECUTIONS

An eerie feature of many of ISIS's execution videos is the relative calm of the individuals about to be executed. In some cases, the hostages have appeared drugged, but in others there are signs that all may not be as it seems. Experts believe that some of the videos are completely staged.[1] In the James Foley video, despite the knife being drawn across his neck several times, there is no sign of blood. The screen fades to black, then returns with the final shot of Foley's body. Either the execution was so badly botched they had to edit it out, or someone besides the now-dead British jihadi who headlined the video did the killing.

A leaked video shows two black-masked ISIS fighters surrounded by camera equipment in front of a giant green screen used for video editing. The existence of this studio, along with some suspect shadows in some videos, suggests that the videos are highly produced affairs where not all is as it seems. It is likely that some hostages are dragged before the camera multiple times and subjected to fake executions, then returned to their cell until the actual execution. Their calmness on camera may be because they have been subjected to several mock executions and believe the current one also to be false. Unfortunately, the final execution is all too real, but the victims do not realize the reality of the situation until it is too late.

serves as a powerful motivation for those who feel marginalized by the Western societies in which they live. Failure to integrate with modern societies in the West has left a generation of Muslims vulnerable to a sense of alienation and a desire to find meaning and some type of personal power. The jihadist hostage videos seem to offer both.

FALL OF MOSUL

They were ten thousand Iraqi forces against three thousand ISIS soldiers, and yet the Iraqi military ran away. The soldiers shed pieces of their uniforms as they fled from a much smaller force. The collapse of the Iraqi Security Forces (ISF) at Mosul, Iraq, was embarrassing for the American military, which had spent a decade training the force. Reports of the strength and capability of the ISF were frequent from military circles, yet the force ran at the first sign of trouble, leaving weapons and vehicles behind. The American equipment gave ISIS a strategic victory, and ISIS paraded through Mosul with its new American equipment.

It is perhaps the greatest example of the propaganda value of ISIS's videos. Why would ten thousand armed and trained soldiers flee in the face of a much smaller force of untrained jihadi militants? Perhaps they were afraid that they would be the stars of the next ISIS execution video.

With its videos, ISIS has created such an aura of strength and brutality that the ISF ran rather than face them and the potential of being captured. Not all of ISIS's enemies run away. Ceylan Ozalp was a nineteen-year-old Kurdish female fighter. In an interview with the BBC, she scoffed at how much fear a female fighter put into the hearts of ISIS. She said, "When they see a woman with a gun, they're so afraid they begin to shake. They portray themselves as tough guys to the world. But when they see us with our guns they run away."[3] While fighting ISIS,

With the war against ISIS still raging in 2017, more and more Iraqi citizens have been forced into refugee camps. Here, an Iraqi soldier is shown helping two displaced children.

her position was overrun on a mountain in northern Syria. She had time to speak to the world one last time before ISIS's forces reached her. "Good-bye," she said, and turned her gun on herself to avoid capture.

TOURISM TROUBLES

ISIS attacks throughout the Middle East have damaged the tourism industry, but the damage is not limited to the Middle East. Attacks in European capitals have hurt the tourism industry there as people are afraid of being victims of the next unexpected attack in a crowded market or building. Tourism dropped by as much as 20 percent in Tunisia, Turkey, France, and Egypt after attacks in those countries.[4] In Syria and Iraq, tourist sites and ancient monuments that have stood for centuries have been destroyed by ISIS in its campaign against anything not representative of Islam.

Tourism makes up 10 percent of the income for the countries of the European Union, which experts estimate have lost more than $1 billion in tourism dollars because of ISIS's attacks on tourist capitals.[5] Meanwhile, countries in the Middle East and North Africa have been hit even harder. Tunisia and Egypt, two countries in the region that rely on tourist dollars, have seen their already fragile economies strangled by ISIS's impact. In Tunisia, hotels, restaurants, and beaches sit empty. Miles of sand along pristine water, once choked with French, German, and British tourists, stand empty except for the occasional mother and child roaming the beach. Restaurants that once required reservations months in advance now send their waiters to the street to beg passing visitors to come in and enjoy a meal. The pyramids in Egypt are sparsely visited, while Nile River cruise boats sit empty along the docks, stacked one against the other like coffins.

From a tiny corner of the deserts in Iraq and Syria, ISIS has lashed out at the entire world. All the world's citizens, capitals, and treasures are at risk in the destructive rise of the terrorist organization. While hostage taking is not a new phenomenon, ISIS has taken it to new levels of brutality. Journalists, aid workers, and the innocent people caught in the path of the group have all found themselves victims of the so-called caliphate's reign of terror. People like James Foley, who sought only to highlight the plight of those caught under ISIS's brutal thumb, have found themselves victims of the violence. Aid workers like

DESTROYING HISTORY

It is a depressing before-and-after picture. The al-Medina market in Aleppo had stood for centuries as the largest covered market in the world. The ancient market is now in shambles after falling victim to the fighting in Syria. Its stalls, once full of gold, perfume, and various spices, now lay in cobwebs, doors torn askew. It was one of six United Nations Educational, Scientific, and Cultural Organization (UNESCO) World Heritage Sites in Syria before the civil war and subsequent rise of ISIS. Now all six of the UNESCO sites, designated as important to the collective interests of humanity,[6] have been destroyed or damaged. Videos of ISIS destroying priceless artifacts and historical sites throughout Iraq and Syria have appeared online, adding to the cultural loss. These ancient sites are unfortunate hostages. Many have suffered the same fate as the people ISIS takes prisoner.

Iraqi army forces joined Kurdish Peshmerga soldiers for a joint operation in November 2014. Together, and with help from the United States, the fighters were able to reclaim Al-Sadiyah in Diyala, Iraq, which had previously been held by ISIS. They are shown holding the Iraqi flag as well as the captured black flag of ISIS.

Kayla Mueller, who only want to ease the suffering, have found themselves suffering even worse fates.

While ISIS is losing ground in Iraq and Syria, it remains a threat that the countries of the world must overcome. The argument continues whether countries and families should pay ransoms or execute daring raids to save hostages.

ISIS has a very clear mission in taking hostages. It takes them for financial gain and for propaganda value. As long as it holds ground in war-torn nations, it will remain a threat. Even after the group is defeated and its lands returned to the people of Iraq and Syria, the group is likely to continue to inspire violence and hostage taking by those who identify with the group's message.

As long as there's someone out there for jihadists to pledge their allegiance to and a fight to be had, citizens of the world who don't believe are at risk of becoming hostages. Whether they're taken as a means of income or a way to spread a message, hostages are a valuable tool for ISIS and the myriad terror groups with which it is affiliated. And ISIS has made the most of every hostage it has taken. From the unknown Yazidi men and women it has captured and killed to the headline-making Westerners who've been its prisoners, ISIS know how to use its hostages to the best advantage, whether that means ISIS is able to strike fear in the hearts of citizens in its newly captured territory, make millions off of ransomed hostages, or spread its message around the world thanks to news coverage of its hostage and execution videos.

Eventually, ISIS will take its final hostage, but until that moment, the world will have to continue combatting the group and deciding whether it's better to save their citizens with ransom payments or deny the terrorists the funds they want.

CHAPTER NOTES

Chapter 1: A Storied Tradition

1. Denise A. Spellberg, *Thomas Jefferson's Qur'an* (New York, NY: Random House, 2013), p. 418.
2. Gardener W. Allen, *Our Navy and the Barbary Corsairs* (Hamden, CT: Archon Books, 1965), pp. 150–151.
3. Elizabeth Huff, "The First Barbary War," The Jefferson Monticello, August 2, 2011, https://www.monticello.org/site/research-and-collections/first-barbary-war.
4. Spellberg, p. 449.
5. Office of the Press Secretary, "Presidential Policy Directive—Hostage Recovery Activities," White House, June 24, 2015, https://obamawhitehouse.archives.gov/the-press-office/2015/06/24/presidential-policy-directive-hostage-recovery-activities.
6. Simon Reeve, *One Day in September: The Full Story of the 1972 Munich Olympics Massacre and the Israeli Revenge Operation "Wrath of God"* (New York, NY: Arcade: 2011).
7. Encyclopedia Britannica (online), "Iran Hostage Crises," January 10, 2017, https://www.britannica.com/event/Iran-hostage-crisis.
8. Jakob Schiller, "Terrorist Hostages' Belongings Reveal the Horrors of Captivity," Wired (online), January 20, 2015, https://www.wired.com/2015/01/glenna-gordon-al-qaeda-and-isis-gostages.
9. Thomas Joscelyn, "Al Qaeda's General Command Disowns the Islamic State of Iraq and the Sham," Long War Journal (online), February 3, 2014, http://www.longwarjournal.org/archives/2014/02/al_qaedas_general_co.php.

Chapter 2: Stranger in a Strange Land

1. David Rohde, "How the US and Europe Failed James Foley," *Atlantic* (online), August 20, 2014, https://www.theatlantic.com/international/archive/2014/08/how-the-us-failed-james-foley/378863.
2. John Lee Anderson, "The Men Who Killed James Foley," *New Yorker* (online), August 20, 2014, http://www.newyorker.com/news/news-desk/men-killed-james-foley.

3. Catherine E. Shoichet, Jason Hanna, and Pamela Brown, "American ISIS Hostage Kayla Mueller Dead, Family Says," CNN, February 11, 2015, http://www.cnn.com/2015/02/10/world/isis-hostage-mueller.

4. Seymour M. Hersh, "Torture at Abu Ghraib," *New Yorker* (online), May 10, 2004, http://www.newyorker.com/magazine/2004/05/10/torture-at-abu-ghraib.

5. BBC.com (online), "US Hostage Kayla Mueller 'Killed by ISIS' say Ex-Slaves," http://www.bbc.com/news/world-middle-east-34205911.

6. Theo Padnos, "My Captivity," *New York Times* (online), October 28, 2014, https://www.nytimes.com/2014/10/28/magazine/theo-padnos-american-journalist-on-being-kidnapped-tortured-and-released-in-syria.html?_r=0.

7. Committee to Protect Journalists, "1231 Journalists Killed Since 1992," February 25, 2017, https://cpj.org/killed.

8. International News Safety Institute, "Journalism Safety: Threats to Media Workers and Measures to Protect Them," February 20, 2014, https://newssafety.org/uploads/Good%20Practice%20INSI%20Final%20Feb2014.pdf.

Chapter 3: **Taking All Comers**

1. The Avalon Project, "The Code of Hammurabi," Yale Law School, 2008, http://avalon.law.yale.edu/ancient/hamframe.asp.

2. Jonah Blank, "Experts React to ISIS's Gruesome Execution of Jordanian Pilot," RAND Corporation, February 4, 2015, http://www.rand.org/blog/2015/02/experts-react-to-isiss-gruesome-execution-of-jordanian.html.

3. Shannon Tiezzi, "ISIS: Chinese Hostage Executed," *Diplomat* (online), November 19, 2015, http://thediplomat.com/2015/11/isis-chinese-hostage-executed.

4. Jennine Liu, "China's ISIS Woes," *Diplomat* (online), February 26, 2016, http://thediplomat.com/2016/02/chinas-isis-woes.

Chapter 4: **On Foreign Soil**

1. BBC.com, "Libya Hotel Attack: Five foreigners among nine killed," January 28, 2015, http://www.bbc.com/news/world-africa-31001094.

2. Mary Beth Sheridan, "Tunisia's Bardo Museum, Attacked by Terrorists, Is Home to Amazing Roman Treasures," *Washington Post* (online),

March 18, 2015, https://www.washingtonpost.com/news/worldviews/ wp/2015/03/18/tunisias-bardo-museum-attacked-by-terrorists-is-home-to-amazing-roman-treasures/?utm_term=.62a92a7d6f7e.

3. France 24, "Paris Attacks What We Know So Far," November 15, 2015, http://www.france24.com/en/20151115-paris-attacks-bataclan-what-we-know-attacker-victims-arrests-belgium.

4. Phillip Connor, "Conflicts in Syria, Iraq and Yemen Lead to Millions of Displaced Migrants in the Middle East Since 2005," Pew Research Center, October 18, 2016, http://www.pewglobal.org/2016/10/18/ conflicts-in-syria-iraq-and-yemen-lead-to-millions-of-displaced-migrants-in-the-middle-east-since-2005.

5. Kathleen Newland, "The U.S. Record Shows Refugees Are Not a Threat," Migration Policy Institute, October 2015, http://www. migrationpolicy.org/news/us-record-shows-refugees-are-not-threat.

6. Julia Amalia Heyer and Petra Truckendanner, "Healing the Scars of Bataclan," Spiegel Online, February 16, 2016, http://www.spiegel.de/ international/europe/paris-terror-attack-victims-struggling-to-come-to-terms-a-1077426.html.

7. Goutham Kandru, "ISIS and the Crusades," Dartmouth University, May 16, 2016, http://sites.dartmouth.edu/ crusadememory/2016/05/16/isis-and-the-crusades.

8. Camila Domonoske, "2 Men Take Hostages, Kill Priest in French Church; Attack Claimed by ISIS," NPR.org, July 26, 2016, http://www .npr.org/sections/thetwo-way/2016/07/26/487475199/two-men-take-hostages-kill-priest-in-french-church-attack-claimed-by-isis.

Chapter 5: Cities Under Siege

1. Mohammed A. Salih, "I Am a 14-year-old Yazidi Girl Given as a Gift to an ISIS Commander. Here's How I Escaped," *Washington Post* (online), September 10, 2014, https://www.washingtonpost.com/posteverything/ wp/2014/09/10/i-am-a-14-year-old-yazidi-girl-given-as-a-gift-to-an-isis-commander-heres-how-i-escaped/?utm_term=.5fbc21f17426.

2. Avi Asher-Schapiro, "Who Are the Yazidis, the Ancient, Persecuted Religious Minority Struggling to Survive in Iraq?" *National Geographic*, August 11, 2014, http://news.nationalgeographic.com/ news/2014/08/140809-iraq-yazidis-minority-isil-religion-history.

3. Kelly Cobiella and Yuka Tachibana, "ISIS Terror: One Yazidi's Battle to Chronicle the Death of a People," MSNBC.com, November 23, 2015, http://www.nbcnews.com/storyline/isis-uncovered/isis-terror-one-yazidis-battle-chronicle-death-people-n461566.

4. Mark Scheffler and Reem Makhoul, "Surreal Scenes of Life under ISIS in Mosul, Iraq," YouTube (video), June 10, 2015, https://www.youtube.com/watch?v=vleBHl82svY.

5. "The U.S. Military's Poor Record Training the Iraqi Army," War Is Boring, January 22, 2016, https://warisboring.com/the-u-s-military-s-poor-record-training-the-iraqi-army-328bee4315a9#.g2prszbtp.

6. Lucy Rodgers, "Inside Mosul: What's Life Like Under Islamic State?" BBC.com, June 9, 2015, http://www.bbc.com/news/world-middle-east-32831854.

7. Mairi Mackay, "'Help Us Find a Life:' The terrifying reality of living under ISIS in Raqqa, Syria," CNN.com, December 4, 2015, http://www.cnn.com/2015/12/04/middleeast/isis-syria-raqqa-life.

Chapter 6: Interpreting God's Will

1. Terrence McCoy and Adam Taylor, "Islamic State Says Immolation Was Justified; Experts on Islam Say No," *Washington Post* (online), February 4, 2015, https://www.washingtonpost.com/news/morning-mix/wp/2015/02/04/the-chilling-reason-the-islamic-state-burned-a-jordanian-pilot-alive/?utm_term=.3122d7e96be0.

2. Ahmad Atif Ahmad, *Islam, Modernity, Violence, and Everyday Life* (New York, NY: Palgrave Macmillan, 2009), p. 164.

3. Taylor McNeil, "The Greater Jihad," *Tufts Journal*, March 2008, http://tuftsjournal.tufts.edu/2008/03/features/04.

4. Maududi, "Period of Revelation," *Introduction of Ad-Dahr* (Lahore, Pakistan: Islamic Press, 1967), p. 159.

5. Al-Islam.org, "Badr, The First Battle in Islam," https://www.al-islam.org/life-muhammad-prophet-sayyid-saeed-akhtar-rizvi/battles.

6. Barnaby Rogerson, *The Prophet Muhammad: A Biography* (New York, NY: Paulist Press, 2003), p. 190.

7. Sami Aboudi and Suleiman Al-Khalidi, "Clerics Denounce Burning Alive as Un-Islamic," Reuters, February 4, 2015, http://uk.reuters.com/article/uk-mideast-crisis-jordan-clerics-idUKKBN0L815F20150204.

8. Jonathan E. Brockopp, "Slaves and Slavery," *Encyclopedia of the Qur'ān*, General editor: Jane Dammen McAuliffe (Washington, DC: Georgetown University Press, 2011).

9. Nour Malas, "Ancient Prophecies Motivate Islamic State Militants: Battlefield Strategies Driven by 1,400-year-old Apocalyptic Ideas," *Wall Street Journal*, November 18, 2014, https://online.wsj.com/articles/ancient-prophecies-motivate-islamic-state-militants-1416357441.

Chapter 7: Free at Last

1. Foxnews.com, "Podesta Leaks Show Clinton Email Linking Saudi Arabia, Qatar to ISIS," October 11, 2016, http://www.foxnews.com/politics/2016/10/11/podesta-leaks-show-clinton-email-linking-saudi-arabia-qatar-to-isis.html.

2. Lawrence Wright, "Five Hostages," *New Yorker*, July 6 and 13, 2015, http://www.newyorker.com/magazine/2015/07/06/five-hostages.

3. Polly Mosendz, "How Qatar Helped Free an American Hostage Without Paying Ransom," *Atlantic*, August 26, 2014, https://www.theatlantic.com/international/archive/2014/08/how-qatar-helped-helped-free-an-american-hostage-without-paying-ransom/379178/.

4. Rukmini Callimachi, "Paying Ransoms, Europe Bankrolls Qaeda Terror," *New York Times* (online), July 29, 2014, https://www.nytimes.com/2014/07/30/world/africa/ransoming-citizens-europe-becomes-al-qaedas-patron.html?_r=0.

5. Callimachi.

6. Ibid.

7. Michael Hastings, "America's Last Prisoner of War," *Rolling Stone*, June 7, 2012, http://www.rollingstone.com/politics/news/americas-last-prisoner-of-war-20120607.

8. Michael R. Gordon and Eric Schmitt, "U.S. Soldier Dies in Raid to Free Prisoners of ISIS in Iraq," *New York Times* (online), October 22, 2015, https://www.nytimes.com/2015/10/23/world/middleeast/us-commandos-iraq-isis.html.

9. Qur'an, Chapter 29, Verse 46, Various translations available at http://corpus.quran.com/translation.jsp?chapter=29&verse=46.

10. Jack Moore, "Isis Releases 43 Assyrian Hostages from Raqqa After Ransom Payments," *Newsweek* (online), February 22, 2106, http://

www.newsweek.com/isis-releases-43-assyrian-hostages-syria-raqqa-ransom-428974.

Chapter 8: **Strategy of Fear**

1. James Gordon Meek, Brian Ross, and Rhonda Schwartz, "ISIS Hostages Likely Faced Mock Executions Before Beheadings, Officials Say," abcnews.com, February 2, 2015, http://abcnews.go.com/International/isis-hostages-faced-mock-executions-beheadings-officials/story?id=28661536.

2. Joshua Berlinger, "The Names: Who Has Been Recruited to ISIS from the West," CNN.com, February 26, 2015, http://www.cnn.com/2015/02/25/world/isis-western-recruits.

3. "Kurdish Female Fighter 'Killed Herself' to Avoid Being ISIS Hostage," al-Arabiya News, October 5, 2014, http://english.alarabiya.net/en/News/middle-east/2014/10/05/Kurdish-female-fighter-killed-herself-to-avoid-being-ISIS-hostage.html.

4. Ben Popken, "Global Tourism Takes Massive Hit After Spike in Terror Attacks," NBC News (online), July 21, 2016, http://www.nbcnews.com/business/travel/global-tourism-takes-massive-hit-after-spike-terror-attacks-n614111.

5. Liz Alderman, "Terrorism Scares Away the Tourists Europe Was Counting On," *New York Times* (online), July 29, 2016, https://www.nytimes.com/2016/07/30/business/international/europe-economy-gdp-terrorism.html.

6. World Heritage Convention, UNESCO, "Selection Criteria," http://whc.unesco.org/en/criteria.

GLOSSARY

Abu Ghraib Currently the Baghdad Central Prison, Abu Ghraib was used by US military forces as a prison for suspects captured in Iraq between 2003 and 2006. In 2004, US guards working at the prison were found to have been torturing prisoners, resulting in a huge scandal for the US military and numerous attacks on the prison.

aid worker An aid worker is typically a volunteer who travels to impoverished or war-torn countries to assist citizens with everything from gaining access to clean water and fresh food to getting medical help.

al-Qaeda This terrorist organization was founded by Osama bin Laden and is now run by Ayman al-Zawahiri; it is a militant Sunni group that was responsible for the September 11, 2001, attacks on the United States.

beheading The act of killing a hostage by cutting off his or her head; barbaric practice used by ISIS and other groups to show their dominance over their enemies.

execution The planned and carefully choreographed murder of an enemy.

Guantánamo Bay A US military prison located on a parcel of land in Cuba that the United States rents from the Cuban government. Prisoners held at Guantánamo, also called Gitmo, are among the most dangerous prisoners held by the US, but there are also prisoners held there who have not been found guilty but whom the US has had trouble finding new homes for.

hostage Someone taken and held against his or her will, typically to be used as a bargaining chip by the captor.

ISIS takes hostages to gain ransom money or to use its victims in propaganda.

human rights violations According to most countries in the world, citizens are guaranteed certain rights, such as fair treatment by governments and access to basic things like food, water, and shelter. Violations of these rights can be committed by governments or terrorist organizations and include such offenses as rape and torture, as well as denying citizens access to things like clean water.

Islamic State Also called ISIS, ISIL, IS, or Da'esh, the Islamic State is a terror group that practices an extreme version of Islam and believes that Muslims should live in their own state, separate from the nonbelievers.

lone wolf Someone who acts on his or her own without being specifically ordered by a leader or group. In terms of terrorism, a lone wolf is an attacker who chooses and carries out his or her own attack in the name of ISIS but who is not directed to do so by ISIS leaders and does not receive support from the greater ISIS organization.

monotheism The belief that there is only one god; Christianity, Judaism, and Islam are all monotheistic faiths.

Muhammad The prophet, or messenger from God, in the Islamic faith, as well as the de facto founder of Islam. Muhammad lived in the seventh century, and in 610 CE, he reported receiving a visit from the angel Gabriel, who delivered to him the word of God.

propaganda Media that aims to promote a specific point of view. ISIS produces propaganda online, through videos posted to social media, as well as through its own magazine, *Dabiq*.

Quran The Islamic holy book. It is believed that the Quran is the word of God as told to Muhammad and written down by Muhammad's scribes.

ransom Money paid for the release of a hostage.

Special Operations Forces Specially trained and equipped military forces that take on missions that require unique skill sets that the general military population doesn't have. Navy SEALs and Army Green Berets are considered Special Operations Forces.

Taliban An extremist Muslim political group that forces followers to obey sharia law.

Wahhabism An ultraconservative version of Islam, Wahhabism is named for its founder, Muhammad ibn Abd al-Wahhab. Wahhab believed that "religious innovation" was wrong and required followers to practice a puritanical version of Islam.

West The West is a catch-all phrase used mostly to mean America, but that also includes Europe and Canada. The name is derived from "western hemisphere," where America and Europe are located. As it regards ISIS, the West is the enemy of the caliphate.

FURTHER READING

Books

Damsgard, Puk, and David Young (translator). *The ISIS Hostage: One Man's True Story of 13 Months in Captivity.* New York, NY: Pegasus Books, 2017.

Gerges, Fawaz A. *ISIS: A History.* Princeton, NJ: Princeton University Press, 2016.

Weiss, Michael, and Hassan Hassan. *ISIS: Inside the Army of Terror.* New York, NY: Regan Arts, 2015.

Websites

Human Rights Watch

www.hrw.org

HRW is a human rights organization that reports on and fights against abuses faced by citizens in countries around the world. In addition to reporting on abuses committed by government organizations, HRW also focuses on the situation in ISIS territory.

United Nations

www.un.org

The United Nations reports on human rights situations around the globe, including covering the ongoing hostage situations in ISIS-held lands.

INDEX

A

Abu Ghraib, 22
Afghanistan, 14, 16, 32, 70, 74
aid workers, 7, 23, 87
American hostages, 11, 75
Army Green Berets, 75

B

Baghdadi, Abu Bakr al, 23
beheadings, 20, 55
Bergdahl, Bowe, 70, 74
Berry, David, 37
Bin Laden, Osama, 16

C

Chinese Muslims, 32–34
Christians, 7, 45, 49, 51, 55, 67, 78

E

Eagles of Death Metal, 39, 43–44

F

Foley, James, 17–19, 26, 35, 82, 87

G

God's law, interpretations, 30, 57–59
Guantánamo Bay, 74

H

Hadith, 51, 53, 58–59, 67
Hamel, Jacques, 44
Hammurabi Code, 30, 65
hostages, 8, 10–11, 13–18, 20, 22, 24, 26–28, 30, 32–41, 67–68, 70–71, 75, 78–82, 87, 90
  bargaining chips, 36
  concubine, 52
  execution, 8, 17, 22, 26, 29, 33–34, 80–82
  exploited, 17
  ransomed, 17–18, 65, 90
  rape, 23, 52
  rescued, 78
hostage situations, 8, 71

I

infidels, 51–52, 61
Iran, 13–14, 16
Iraq, 8, 17, 22, 25, 27, 30–33, 35, 49–50, 75–76, 78–79, 83, 86–88, 90
Iraqi Security Forces (ISF), 56, 75, 83–84
ISIL (Islamic State of Iraq and the Levant), 7
ISIS (Islamic State of Iraq and Syria), 9, 17–18, 20–21, 23–24, 26–39, 43–45, 48–49, 51–59, 65–68, 75–76, 78–81, 83–84, 86–88, 90

caliphate, 8, 57, 61, 78, 81
legal code, 53
medieval code, 49
ISIS fighters, 51–53, 63, 75
Islam, 11, 24, 34, 52, 55, 58–59,
61, 64, 67, 86
Islamic law, 58, 65
Israel, 21, 27, 74

J

journalists, 18–19, 21, 25, 34, 87
sexual assault, 25

K

Kasasbeh, al-, 27, 29, 65
kidnappings, 17, 67–68
Kurdish fighters, 56, 75
female fighters, 83
Kurdish forces, 8, 75–76, 78

M

Mueller, Kayla, 20–21, 23, 70,
90
Muhammad, 30, 58–59, 61,
64–65
Munich Olympics Massacre, 15
Muslims, 32, 45, 55, 58, 61,
64–65, 67, 81, 83
Muslim scholars, 57, 67

N

negotiating, 13, 16, 18, 24,
70–71

O

Obama, President Barack, 19

orange prison jumpsuits, 22
Ottosen, Daniel Rye, 34–35

P

Padnos, Theo, 24, 70
prison, 18, 22, 24, 34, 52, 75, 78
prisoners, 12, 22, 24, 34, 51, 55,
59, 61, 65, 74–75, 78, 87, 90
propaganda, 8, 29, 78

Q

Qaeda, al-, 7, 17, 68
Quran, 24, 30, 51, 58–61, 65,
67

R

raid, daring helicopter, 75
refugees, 21, 39, 41, 93

S

Saudi Arabia, 30, 60, 64
slave market, 21
slaves, 10, 30, 52, 61, 66–67
soldiers, female, 76
Sunna, 53, 59, 67
Sunnis, 56
Syria, 8, 18–19, 21, 23–28,
31–35, 41, 44, 49, 54–55, 57,
78–79, 81, 86–87, 90
Syrians, 8–9, 78

T

terror, 8, 18, 27, 35, 37, 44, 49,
80, 87
terrorist groups, 8, 17, 49, 68,
71, 78–80

terrorist organizations, 24–25,
27, 70, 87
terrorist plots, 41
terrorists, 13, 15–16, 18, 25,
37–41, 70–71, 74–75, 78, 90
torture, 21, 22, 34
tourism industry, 80, 86
fear, 15, 18, 80–81, 83, 85,
87, 90
Tripoli, 10–11, 13, 36, 38

U

Uighurs, 31–32, 34

W

Wahhabism, 60, 99

Y

Yazidis, 21, 49–51, 53, 66–67,
93
devil-worshippers, 50
Malek Taus, 49